Wolf Hill

Blaze!

Roderick Hunt

Illustrated by Alex Brychta

OXFORD UNIVERSITY PRESS

Great Clarendon Street, Oxford OX2 6DP

Oxford University Press is a department of the University of Oxford.
It furthers the University's objective of excellence in research, scholarship,
and education by publishing worldwide in

Oxford New York

Auckland Bangkok Buenos Aires Cape Town Chennai
Dar es Salaam Delhi Hong Kong Istanbul Karachi Kolkata
Kuala Lumpur Madrid Melbourne Mexico City Mumbai Nairobi
São Paulo Shanghai Singapore Taipei Tokyo Toronto

with an associated company in Berlin

First published 2002

British Library Cataloguing in Publication Data

Data available

ISBN 0 19 919526 9

1 3 5 7 9 10 8 6 4 2

Printed in Hong Kong

Chapter 1

The little dog, Max, had run off. He had chased after a rabbit. Gizmo and his dad had called him, but Max had not come back.

Gizmo's dad was worried. 'I hope we haven't lost him,' he said.

Looking after someone else's dog had not been easy.

Max had run into the gorse and thick bushes that grew all the way up the hill.

'He could be anywhere,' said Mr Harding.

'I'll go and look for him,' said Gizmo.

He set off down one of the narrow overgrown paths, calling for Max.

Then he heard something moving among the tangled scrub.

Gizmo pushed his way carefully through the dense dry gorse and brambles.

And that was when he found the secret place.

Chapter 2

Deep among the gorse was a dip in the ground – a small, round, grassy clearing. It couldn't be seen from the path.

Gizmo felt completely alone, cut off from the world. He could see nobody. Nobody could see him.

He lay down on the soft grass and looked up at the sky.

'This is special,' he said. 'It's a secret place.'

As he lay there, Max came running out of the brambles. His coat was covered in burrs and grass seeds. He sat panting next to Gizmo.

Gizmo put his hand on Max's collar.

'You silly dog,' he said. 'You're just trouble on four legs.'

Gizmo picked his way out of the clearing with Max on his lead.

'I'll come back here,' he said.

He didn't know that next time the clearing would become a frightening and dangerous place.

Chapter 3

A week later Gizmo went back with Kat, Loz, and Chris.

Gizmo's mum and dad took them. They were going to pick blackberries while Gizmo and his friends had a picnic in the little clearing.

Gizmo couldn't wait to show the others his secret place. They began to run up the hill.

'Come back!' called Mr Harding. 'I'm not carrying your picnic things.'

They set off again, taking their sandwiches and drinks.

Half way up the hill, they met two teenagers. Gizmo's heart sank. He didn't like the look of them.

They looked like the kind of teenagers who were out to make trouble.

Chapter 4

The teenagers both lit cigarettes.

'Oh look,' said one, blowing out smoke. 'It's a kiddies' picnic.'

The other grabbed the bag of drinks Chris was carrying and swung it round and round.

Mr Harding saw this happen. He shouted at the teenagers. They dropped the bag and ran off.

'It's a good job we're here,' said Mrs Harding.

'I didn't like those big kids,' said Loz. 'They were smoking. I'm glad they've gone.'

They all walked together up the hill.

'This is a good place to pick blackberries,' said Mr Harding, 'so you'll know where we are.'

Gizmo pointed. 'We'll be just up here,' he said. 'Come on!'

He led the others up a narrow, overgrown path.

'Ouch!' called Kat. The arm of her jumper had caught on a bramble. 'It's all sharp and prickly.'

'It gets worse,' laughed Gizmo.

'Is it much farther?' asked Chris. 'This bag is heavy.'

'It's in here,' said Gizmo. Then he frowned. The last time, it had been hard to find a way into the clearing. Now it looked as if a narrow path had been beaten into it.

Someone else had found Gizmo's secret place.

Chapter 5

They pushed their way through to the clearing. Gizmo gasped.

Someone had found the place, all right. There was a pony tied up in the middle of it. It was enjoying the soft grass.

Beside it was a bucket of water.

The pony flicked its head and moved towards them. Gizmo jumped back. He didn't like horses.

Kat pushed past him and stroked the pony's muzzle. 'Oh, it's sweet,' she said. 'I wonder what its name is.'

Loz had some mints. She held one out on the palm of her hand. The pony gently took it and crunched it up.

Gizmo was upset. With a pony in his secret place, they couldn't have the picnic there.

'Let's go somewhere else,' he said with a sigh.

Chapter 6

Chris finished the last sandwich. 'You can see for miles up here,' he said.

They were having their picnic at the top of the hill.

'I can see Wolf Hill School,' said Kat, pointing to the town in the distance.

Then Loz saw something else. 'Look!' she shouted.

Thick white smoke was rising up from lower down the hill.

Mr Harding ran up. 'The gorse is on fire,' he gasped.

Flames began to leap in the air. They could see the fire slowly spreading out like a fan at the bottom of the hill.

Even though they were a long way off, they could hear it crackling.

Chapter 7

Smoke had started to drift towards them. They could smell it in the air.

'There's gorse and scrub all round us. We should get off the hill,' said Mr Harding.

Mrs Harding took out her mobile phone. 'I'll call the fire service,' she said.

Suddenly Kat shouted. ‘The pony! It could be in danger. What if the fire spreads across that way?’

She began to run down towards the little clearing.

Loz and Gizmo ran after her. ‘We’re coming, too,’ called Loz.

‘Come back!’ shouted Mr Harding.

Chapter 8

Loz and Kat reached the clearing first. The pony was jumpy. It could sense something was wrong. It tossed its head up as if trying to get free.

'Steady! Steady!' called Kat. She grabbed the pony's halter.

Seconds later Mr Harding and Gizmo came into the clearing.

'I can't untie the knot,' said Loz. 'It's too tight.'

Smoke began to drift across them.

'We need to be quick,' said Mr Harding. He handed Gizmo a penknife. 'Cut the rope,' he said. 'I'll hold the pony's head.'

It took Gizmo a few seconds to cut through the rope. Mr Harding and Kat led the pony out of the clearing.

Gizmo began to wheeze. The smoke had brought on his asthma.

Chapter 9

The fire was spreading rapidly through the dry gorse. The flames were rising higher and higher. Flakes of white ash blew across in the smoke.

'The fire is coming this way,' said Loz.

'We'll have to run,' shouted Kat.

Gizmo was finding it hard to move. His asthma was worse.

'My inhaler's with the picnic things,' he wheezed. 'I can't run.'

Kat had an idea. 'Sit on the pony,' she said. 'Then we can move fast.'

Mrs Harding and Chris were waiting for them.

'It's safe to go down this path,' said Mrs Harding. 'The fire's moving away from us here.'

In the distance, they heard the sound of fire engines.

Then they heard a woman shouting.

'Oh! You've rescued Blaze,' she called. 'I was terrified he'd be caught in the fire.'

Chapter 10

The fire had left the hillside scarred black.

Mr Harding spoke to an officer. 'We saw some lads smoking up here,' he told her. 'That might have started the fire.'

‘So much for my secret place,’ said Gizmo.

Kat smiled. ‘But if you hadn’t found the clearing, we would never have rescued Blaze.’

'Blaze's owner says we can come back and ride him,' said Loz. 'That will be great.'

Gizmo wasn't so sure. 'I've had my ride,' he grinned.

'And we certainly had a blaze,' said Chris.